Collins

easy learning

English

Ages 3–5

c _ t

m _ t

How to use this book

- Find a quiet, comfortable place to work, away from distractions.

- Tackle one topic at a time.

- Help with reading the instructions where necessary and ensure that your child understands what to do.

- Discuss with your child what they have learnt.

- Let your child return to their favourite pages once they have been completed, to talk about the activities.

- Reward your child with plenty of praise and encouragement.

- There are three ways of learning letters: the way we say the English alphabet in its order a–z; the way we learn to write the letters, grouping letters that are formed in a similar way like c, o, a, d, g, then the letters like i, r, n, m; and lastly when learning phonics we start with s, a, t, p, i, n, then m, d, g, k, c. This book follows the phonics order for single sounds in the first section where letters are spoken using their phonetic sound and the writing order in the second section where letters are written.

Special features

- Parent's notes: These are divided into 'What you need to know', which explain the key English idea, and 'Taking it further', which suggest activities and encourage discussion with your child about what they have learnt.

Published by Collins
An imprint of HarperCollinsPublishers
1 London Bridge Street
London SE1 9GF

Browse the complete Collins catalogue at
www.collins.co.uk

© HarperCollinsPublishers Limited 2006
This edition © HarperCollinsPublishers 2015

11

ISBN 978-0-00-813420-4

Printed in Great Britain by Bell and Bain Ltd, Glasgow

The publisher wishes to thank the following for permission to use copyright material:
p16 © MisterElements/Shutterstock.com, © owatta/Shutterstock.com; p17 © Matthew Cole/Shutterstock.com, © pichayasri/Shutterstock.com, © Sarawut Padungkwan/Shutterstock.com; p18 © robodread/Shutterstock.com

British Library Cataloguing in Publication Data

A Catalogue record for this publication is available from the British Library

Design and layout by Lodestone Publishing Limited and Contentra Technologies
Illustrated by Rachel Annie Bridgen;
www.shootingthelight.com
Handwriting artwork by Kathy Baxendale
Cover design by Sarah Duxbury and Paul Oates
Project managed by Sonia Dawkins
Contributor: Carol Medcalf

Contents

Find and say s, a, t, p, i

- Find and say s in   sun   six   snake

- Find and say a in   ant   apple   ambulance

- Find and say t in   tap   tent   telephone

- Find and say p in   pin   path   penguin

- Find and say i in   ink   insect   inside

What you need to know   Encourage your child to sound out the initial sound of each word, for example by saying the sound 'a' as in 'apple'.

Find and say n, m, d, g, o

- Find and say n in   net   nut   nest

- Find and say m in   mouse   money   moon

- Find and say d in   dog   dish   duck

- Find and say g in   girl   gate   ghost

- Find and say o in   off   orange   octopus

Taking it further   Play 'I Spy' with words beginning with the alphabet sounds. Look out for the letters on packets of food. (Keep to the short vowel sounds, as in ant, egg, ink, orange, umbrella, and avoid the long vowel sounds, as in alien, easy, ice cream, oats, uniform.)

Find and say c, k, e, u, r

- Find and say c in   cat   cow   cup

- Find and say k in   king   kite   key

- Find and say e in   egg   elephant   envelope

- Find and say u in   up   under   umbrella

- Find and say r in   run   rabbit   ring

Find and say h, b, f, l, j

- Find and say h in   hat   hen   house

- Find and say b in   bed   bat   ball

- Find and say f in   fish   feather   finger

- Find and say l in   lamp   lion   letter

- Find and say j in   jam   jug   jelly

Find and say v, w, x, y, z, q

- Find and say v in   vase   violin   vulture

- Find and say w in   web   wave   window

- Find and say x in   fox   six   wax

- Find and say y in   yellow   yoyo   yolk

- Find and say z in   zebra   zzz   zip

- Find and say q in   queen   question   quick

Trace and write c, o, a, d, g

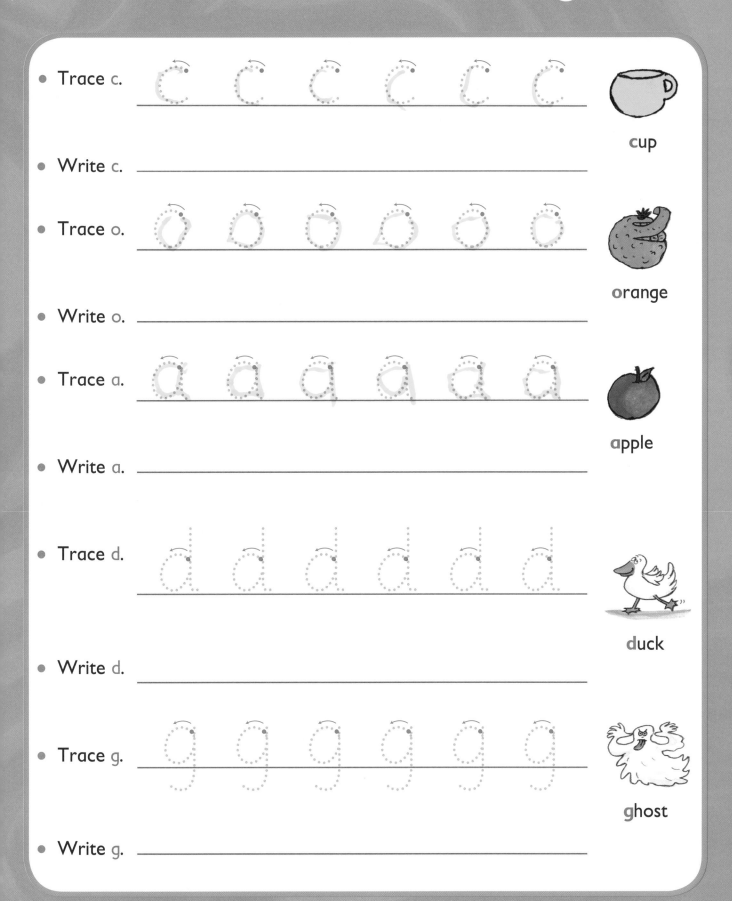

- Trace c.   c c c c c c

cup

- Write c.

- Trace o.   o o o o o o

orange

- Write o.

- Trace a.   a a a a a a

apple

- Write a.

- Trace d.   d d d d d d

duck

- Write d.

- Trace g.   g g g g g g

ghost

- Write g.

What you need to know   Your child can first trace the letter with their finger, then write it in the air and finally trace over the letter with a pencil to join the dots. Then they can try writing the letter with no guiding dots. If your child finds writing the letters hard, start with the letters they find easy and return to the harder ones as their pencil control increases.

Trace and write i, r, n, m, j

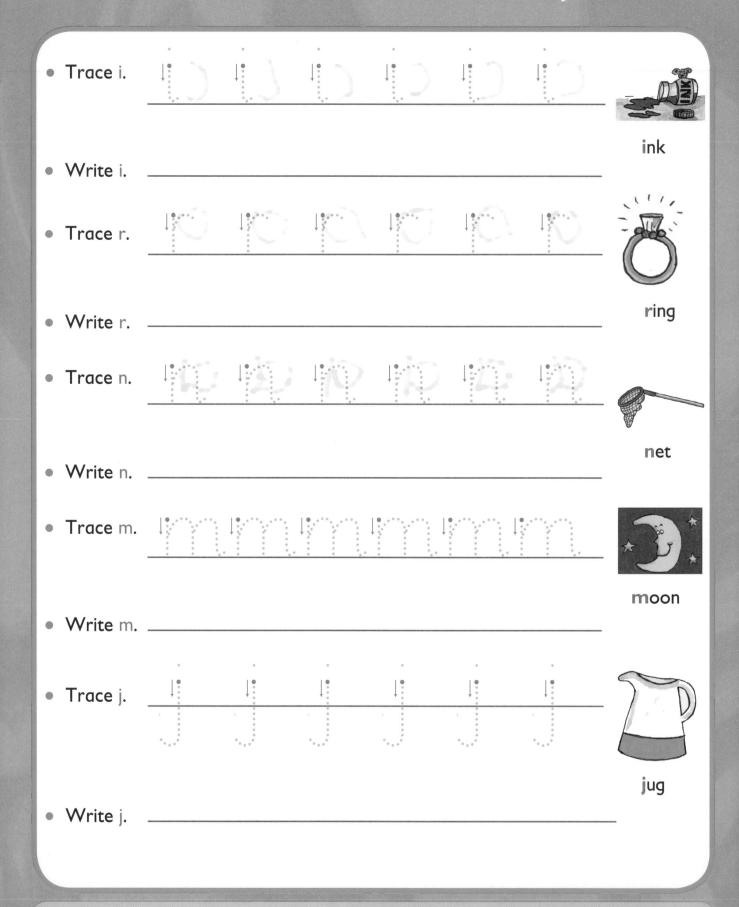

- Trace i.

- Write i.

- Trace r.

- Write r.

- Trace n.

- Write n.

- Trace m.

- Write m.

- Trace j.

- Write j.

ink

ring

net

moon

jug

Taking it further   Provide plenty of writing opportunities with pens and paper. Writing with fingers in sand, flour or paint is great practice too and lots of fun. The size of the letters is not important at this stage, but it will help later on if the letters are formed correctly.

Trace and write l, t, h, k, f

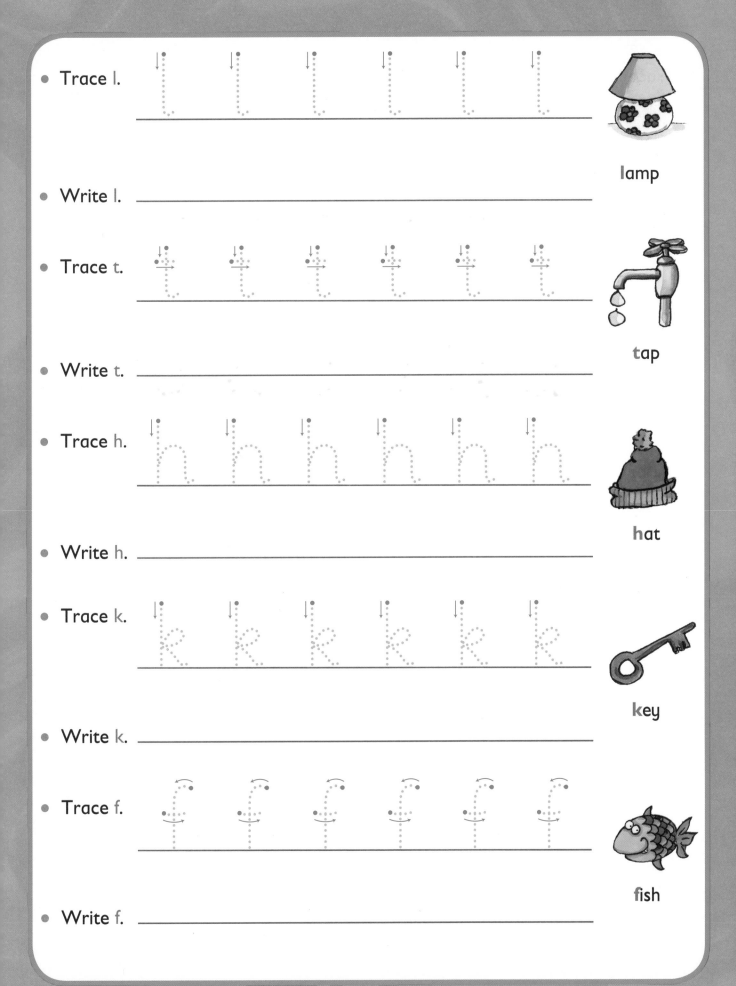

- Trace l.

- Write l. _____

lamp

- Trace t.

- Write t. _____

tap

- Trace h.

- Write h. _____

hat

- Trace k.

- Write k. _____

key

- Trace f.

- Write f. _____

fish

Trace and write b, s, e, q, p

- Trace b.

- Write b.

- Trace s.

- Write s.

- Trace e.

- Write e.

- Trace q.

- Write q.

- Trace p.

- Write p.

ball

sun

elephant

queen

penguin

Trace and write y, u, v, w, x, z

- Trace y.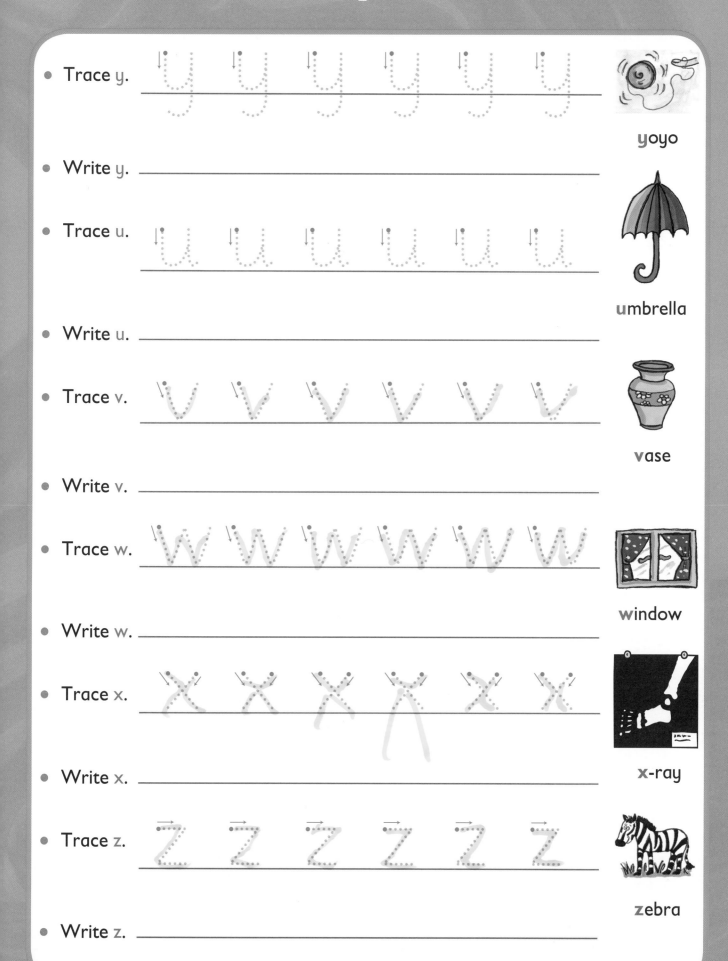

- Write y.

- Trace u.

- Write u.

umbrella

- Trace v.

- Write v.

vase

- Trace w.

- Write w.

window

- Trace x.

- Write x.

x-ray

- Trace z.

zebra

- Write z.

yoyo

13

Alphabetical order

- Trace the whole alphabet.

a b c d e f g h i j k l m n
o p q r s t u v w x y z

- Trace the letters and fill the gaps.

a b c d e f g h i j k l m
o p q r s t u v w x y z

What you need to know Now you have looked at every letter of the alphabet, here they are altogether. Learning which letter comes before or after another will help your child as they start to use the alphabet to order things such as friends' names in registers, or to find addresses in phones or books. If you go to the library, discuss how the books or films are filed and logged.

- Join the food to the letter sound that each one starts with. Maybe you can think of a food item for every letter of the alphabet.

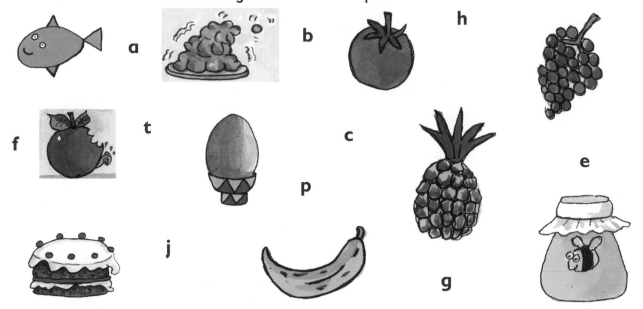

a

b

h

f

t

c

e

p

j

g

- Follow the alphabet to join the dots. Start at the letter a.

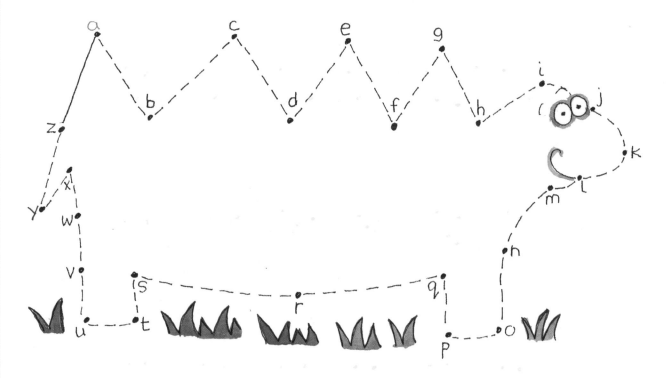

Finish colouring the picture.

ck, ff, ll

- Say **ck** in

Find **ck** in   clock   sack   duck

Trace and write.   clo    sa ___ ___   du ___ ___

- Say **ff** in

Find **ff** in   giraffe   muffin   puffin

Trace and write.   gira ___ ___ e   mu ___ ___ in   pu ___ ___ in

- Say **ll** in

Find **ll** in   bell   doll   ball

Trace and write.   be ___ ___   do ___ ___   ba ___ ___

What you need to know The pairs of letters ck, ff and ll are the first double letter sounds we teach children. The two letters together make one sound. These sounds are found in lots of words.

ss, qu, zz

- Say **ss** in

Find **ss** in   dre**ss**   cro**ss**   gla**ss**

Trace and write.   dre ___ ___   cro ___ ___   gla ___ ___

- Say **qu** in

Find **qu** in   **qu**een   **qu**arter   **qu**estion

Trace and write.   ___ ___ een   ___ ___ arter   ___ ___ estion

- Say **zz** in

Find **zz** in   fi**zz**   pu**zz**le   bu**zz**

Trace and write.   fi ___ ___   pu ___ ___ le   bu ___ ___

What you need to know   These are the next long sounds that children usually learn during the first year of school. Remember that the two letters together make one sound, as heard in the words above. Emphasise the sound as you say each word.

ch, th, ng

- Say **ch** in

  Find **ch** in   **ch**eese   wat**ch**   **ch**air

  Trace and write.   _ _ _ eese   wat _ _   _ _ air

- Say **th** in

  Find **th** in   ba**th**   **th**umb   too**th**

  Trace and write.   ba _ _   _ _ umb   too _ _

- Say **ng** in

  Find **ng** in   ki**ng**   si**ng**   ri**ng**

  Trace and write.   ki _ _   si _ _   ri _ _

Build words with a

- Fill in the missing letter a.

cat

h __ t

m __ t

pan

f __ n

r __ n

- Fill in the two missing letters.

c __ __

m __ __

f __ __

r __ __

h __ __

p __ __

What you need to know   Talk about how these words rhyme: cat, hat, mat. See if your child can add any more words, such as bat, pat, sat. Do the same with pan, fan, ran (can, man, van).

Build words with e

Fill in the missing letter e.

net

p __ t

w __ t

hen

p __ n

t __ n

Fill in the two missing letters.

n __ __

p __ __

h __ __

t __ __

w __ __

p __ __

What you need to know   These 3-letter words are called CVC (**c**onsonant – **v**owel – **c**onsonant) words. They are the first words that children can begin to build from the individual letters.

Build words with i

- Fill in the missing letter i.

pin

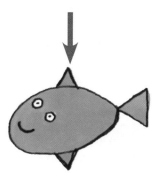

f __ n

t __ n

zip

p __ p

l __ p

- Fill in the two missing letters.

p __ __

l __ __

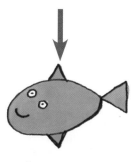

f __ __

z __ __

t __ __

p __ __

Build words with o

- Fill in the missing letter o.

dog

l __ g

f __ g

hot

c __ t

p __ t

- Fill in the two missing letters.

l __ __

p __ __

f __ __

h __ __

d __ __

c __ __

Build words with u

- Fill in the missing letter u.

mug

r __ g

j __ g

sun

b __ n

r __ n

- Fill in the two missing letters.

j __ __

b __ __

s __ __

r __ __

m __ __

r __ __

Taking it further   Think of more words that rhyme with the lists above: mug, rug, jug, bug, hug, tug, etc.

Rhymes

- Say the −at rhymes. Join them to the **hat**.

  cat

  mat

  hat

- Say the −en rhymes. Join them to the **hen**.

  pen

  ten

  hen

- Say the −in rhymes. Join them to the **tin**.

  pin

  fin

  tin

- Say the −ot rhymes. Join them to the **cot**.

  hot

  pot

  cot

- Say the −ug rhymes. Join them to the **mug**.

  jug

  rug

  mug

What you need to know Rhyming is an important way of recognising the spelling pattern of similar words, for example recognising that all the **−at** words are spelt with the same ending.

- Fill the hat with **–at** rhymes.

hat

_ _ _

_ _ _

- Fill the hen with **–en** rhymes.

hen

_ _ _

_ _ _

- Fill the tin with **–in** rhymes.

tin

_ _ _

_ _ _

- Fill the cot with **–ot** rhymes.

cot

_ _ _

_ _ _

- Fill the mug with **–ug** rhymes.

mug

_ _ _

_ _ _

Taking it further Recite nursery rhymes together, emphasising the rhyming words at the end of the lines.

25

Reading with sounds

- Say the letter sounds to read the words.

  Once you can read the word colour each box a different colour.

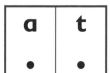  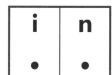 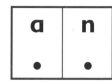

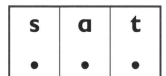 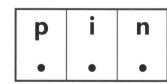

- Say the letter sounds to read the words.

  Colour in all the real words.

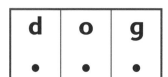 

Tricky words

Some words do not make the phonic sound you have learnt.
These are tricky words that you need to learn to recognise.

- Learn these words.

th	e
_	•

t	o
•	•

I
•

g	o
•	•

n	o
•	•

- Read these words and match them to the right picture.

d	o	g
•	•	•

c	a	t
•	•	•

m	a	t
•	•	•

p	i	n
•	•	•

c	o	t
•	•	•

m	o	p
•	•	•

Taking it further   Make up more real and nonsense words using other letters your child has learnt. You can make letter cards, with one lower case letter on each card, to move around and make up words.

Capital letters

- Trace and copy the capital letters.

A A B B C C D D E E

F F G G H H I I J J

K K L L M M N N O O

P P Q Q R R S S T T

U U V V W W X X

Y Y Z Z

- Join the matching capital and small case letters.

W

A   f   S   s

h   a   F   w

c   C   e

C   H   P   E   p

What you need to know Children should know that capital letters are used for names. They should be able to write their own name. Once they are familiar with all the small letters, they should write the alphabet in capitals.

We use capital letters for names.

- Copy and say these names.

Dan   Beth   Kim   Tom   Gus

— — —   — — — —   — — —   — — —   — — —

Write your name. _____

Write your brother or sister's name. _____

Write your best friend's name. _____

Taking it further   Help your child to write names on birthday cards, invitations and postcards.

29

Words and sentences

• Find words to make sentences.

I	go	come	went	up
you	day	was	look	are
the	of	we	this	dog
me	like	going	big	she
and	they	my	see	on
away	mum	it	at	play
no	yes	for	a	dad
can	he	am	all	is
cat	get	said	to	in

I play with my —— —— ——.

I play with —— —— —— —— ——.

Mum said —— —— ——.

- Now write your own sentences, using just the words in the grid on page 30.

_____

_____

_____

_____

- Draw a picture for one of your sentences.

High frequency words

- Colour each box when you can read and write the word.

I	go	come	went	up
you	day	was	look	are
the	of	we	this	dog
me	like	going	big	she
and	they	my	see	on
away	mum	it	at	play
no	yes	for	a	dad
can	he	am	all	is
cat	get	said	to	in